PARKS AND GARDENS

Michael Chinery

KINGFISHER BOOKS

Parks and Gardens

Our parks and gardens are entirely artificial, but you can still learn a great deal about natural history by studying the plant and animal life in them. Take a good look at the illustration on the right and you will see just how rich in wildlife a park or garden can become. Look at the wide range of habitats that have been created: lawns, paths, walls and fences, shrubberies and trees, ponds, flower beds and vegetable plots. Most of these have their natural equivalents in the wild and it is not surprising that wild plants and animals quickly move in.

Park and garden walls, for instance, are similar to rocky hillsides and coastal cliffs as a habitat. The old walls in the park in the picture are covered with wild plants, such as wallflowers, which grow wild on cliffs. Several birds also make their homes on walls, like the house martin here which tucks its nest under the eaves of the house. House martins still nest on cliffs and rocky places in the wild, but far more of them now nest on buildings. They may be even more common now than they were in earlier times when there were fewer houses. The same is true of the swallow which used to nest mainly in caves but now nests almost entirely in buildings. It likes more cover than the house martin and its favourite nesting sites are buildings with fairly wide entrances, such as barns, covered markets and railway stations. House sparrows and pigeons will nest on buildings even in the busiest parts of town.

Only in parks and gardens can you find so many different habitats in such small areas – perhaps only a few square metres in a town garden. Each habitat has its own assortment of wildlife. Count the different kinds of animals you can find in the illustration here. You'll catch sight of many of them in your own garden or local park, although you are unlikely to find them all at one time. Parks and gardens are obviously very important havens for wildlife, and they could become even more important in the future as more and more of the countryside is built on.

Investigating the Habitats

In the following pages we will explore all these different habitats. All you will need in the way of equipment is a notebook in which to record your observations. A hand lens for close examinations and binoculars for watching birds and other animals from a distance (see page 24) will also be useful. There are plenty of ways in which you can make your own garden especially attractive to wildlife. Butterflies and other insects, for example, will appreciate lots of nectar-filled flowers, while many birds enjoy berry-bearing shrubs in the autumn. You can also provide extra food for the birds in the winter and encourage them to nest in the garden by putting up nesting boxes. Make your garden as varied as possible and you will always have plenty of wildlife to watch.

Garden Birds

The Birds in Your Garden

The birds pictured on this page are some of the many kinds that you might see in your garden. Some of them may actually nest in the trees and shrubs, or even on your house, while others merely come for food. You can increase the number and variety of visitors by putting out food in the autumn and winter. It is well worth buying a seed mixture specially chosen for wild birds. These mixtures contain seeds of many sizes and please a wide variety of birds. Crush some of the seeds with a rolling pin before putting them out: this will make them more attractive to robins and other slender-billed birds. Peanuts – not salted – threaded on strings or put into little net bags are thoroughly enjoyed by the tits and greenfinches.

Most kinds of table scraps are accepted by the birds. You can put them on the bird table just as they are, but it is more fun to mix them into a bird pudding. Pour melted dripping or other fat over the scraps in a basin and leave the mixture to set. Then turn it out on the bird table and watch the birds queuing up to feed. Mix some oatmeal and dried fruit with the scraps to make the pudding even more nourishing.

Feeding Birds

The traditional bird table will attract lots of birds to your garden, A baffle will prevent rats and squirrels from climbing and stealing the food and hurting the birds. Try hanging up a fresh coconut for blue tits and great tits. Fill the shell with bird pudding when the coconut has gone. Put bird pudding and peanuts into holes drilled in a small log. Tits and woodpeckers will enjoy this. Don't forget water for bathing and drinking.

Table · Coconut · Small log · Baffle · Water

COMMON BIRDS

Redstart — male — female

Black Redstart — male — female

Collared Dove

Hoopoe (rare in Britain)

Cuckoo

Wren

Jackdaw

You don't have to be good at woodwork to make a bird table. A piece of wood about 30 centimetres long and 20 centimetres wide nailed to the top of a sturdy post makes a perfectly good table, but you should put an edge around it to stop the food from blowing off. Some people like to add a roof, but this is certainly not necessary. Position the table where you can see it from your window, but not right in the middle of the lawn: the birds like to stay fairly near the shelter of a hedge or bush. The table should be at least 1·5 metres high, so that cats cannot jump on to it. If you live in a town or city and have no suitable place to erect a standard bird table you might be able to fix a feeding tray to a wall or window sill.

Keep a record of all the birds that come to your table. Experiment with the food you provide and try to discover what sort of food each kind of bird prefers. A few birds, including the dunnock and the blackbird, prefer to take their food on the ground, so throw some of the food down for them.

Song Thrush

Dunnock

female

House Sparrow

Italian Sparrow (male)

male

Starling

Blackbird

Great Tit

female

male

Greenfinch

Robin

Blue Tit

House Martin

winter

Magpie

summer

Pied Wagtail

Swallow

City Birds

Blackbirds are especially fond of apples in the winter. Gradually cut down on feeding when the birds begin to nest in spring. There are plenty of natural foods around at this time and they are much better for the baby birds. Don't put out peanuts in the spring, but if you can get some mealworms from a pet shop your robin will be very grateful and may even take them from your hand.

Most birds like fruit, and you can encourage them into your garden by planting berry-bearing bushes such as cotoneasters and guelder roses. Honeysuckle also produces good fruits, and its flowers attract moths at night. Bushes also encourage birds to nest in your garden. Look at page 29 to discover how to make artificial homes for your garden birds as well.

City Birds

The birds that visit your garden can also be seen in town parks – which are really just big gardens. As long as there are some trees and bushes, you will find plenty of birds. But some birds manage to live right in the middle of our towns, where there is often no plant life of any kind. The best known of these city-dwellers is the town pigeon, shown on the page opposite. Watch how it struts along the pavements, pecking away at anything that looks as if it could be edible. This bird is not frightened of people and in some places, such as London's Trafalgar Square, you can see thousands of pigeons landing on tourists' hands and eagerly taking popcorn and any other food on offer.

Birds also gather around street markets, where lots of fruit and vegetable scraps fall to the ground. Railway stations and yards also provide plenty of food, accidentally dropped by passengers or spilt from grain wagons.

Town pigeons are descended from the wild rock dove that lives on rocky hillsides and sea cliffs. The rock dove has been domesticated

Below: A huge flock of starlings darkens the sky as it comes in to roost on a city's trees and buildings on a winter afternoon. If you live in the country watch out for small starling flocks linking up as they fly to the roost.

for centuries – for food, for racing or for show – and many birds inevitably escaped to take up residence in our towns. Millions now live in towns and cities nearly all over the world. Notice the great variation in colour, from the natural grey to black, brown and white: many are multicoloured. This variation is due to the many fancy varieties, bred by bird fanciers, that have escaped over the years to join the town flocks. Most birds still retain the natural pink patch on the neck and the white rump which you can see as they fly up. Listen to the call of the town pigeon: *oo-roo-cooooo*, with the last syllable loud and long. This is quite different from the *cu-coo-cu* of the collared dove (see page 4) which has a long middle syllable. The collared dove does not live in the middle of the town, but often mingles with the town pigeon in parks.

You won't have to search very hard to find the other major city bird, the house sparrow. This bird is essentially a seed-eater, but it thrives on all sorts of food that people may drop. The house sparrow is a little less common in city centres than it was in the days of horse-drawn transport, when the horses spilt grain all over the streets, but you can still see large numbers of these birds at railway yards and stations and around the docks. It makes its untidy nest in any convenient crevice. House sparrows are also abundant in parks and gardens. They are fond of company and usually move about in small flocks. The tree sparrow is similar to the house sparrow but the top of its head is brown. Look at the picture of the dunnock on page 5: can you see how this garden bird differs from the house sparrow? The large numbers of sparrows living in cities attract the kestrels. These speckled birds of prey sometimes nest on window sills and other high ledges in city centres.

On winter afternoons the city skyline may be darkened by huge flocks of starlings flying in to roost after a day spent feeding in gardens or open country. The flocks come from all directions and sleep together in their thousands. They use the same trees or buildings night after night and they are

The Aggressive Robin

Robins stake out their territories in the autumn and keep other robins out with their loud songs and aggressive behaviour. If you have a resident robin you can watch this behaviour by setting up a model robin. It need not be a very good model as long as it has a red breast. Your garden robin will attack it several times until it realizes that the model is harmless. Female robins move into the males' territories in the winter ready for nesting, but not without a few skirmishes.

The Town Pigeon

Town pigeons are quite happy to nest on buildings and even on statues, for these are not really very different from their original homes on the cliffs. Because their droppings disfigure buildings and monuments, their presence is not always welcome.

extremely noisy before they settle down. Their droppings also damage the trees and buildings. You won't see the flocks leave in the morning because the birds fly off singly or in small groups. It is thought that the extra warmth of the city attracts the starlings to these regular roosting places.

Garden Flowers

Garden Flowers

Have you ever wondered where our garden flowers and vegetables come from? You don't see them growing wild in the countryside. Many of them have been introduced from other countries: dahlias from Mexico, chrysanthemums from the Far East, and runner beans from South America. Many others are descended from native plants, but these may have changed so much that the original plants are no longer recognizable. Plant breeders used to take seeds from the biggest and brightest flowers each year, and gradually produced bigger and bigger flowers. They now pollinate the flowers of one variety with pollen from another to produce hybrids. These may look quite different from the original plants and it is difficult to say what their wild ancestors were. But you can see the resemblances in some cases: it is easy to see that the garden pansy has come from the little field pansy and the polyanthus still has many features in common with the wild primrose.

Garden Weeds

Weeds are simply plants growing where we don't want them. Some are foreign plants that have found their way over here and made a nuisance of themselves. Oxford ragwort, for example, is a native of Sicily and was taken to the Oxford Botanic Garden in the 18th century. Seeds soon escaped and the plant is now a common weed, especially in towns. It grows by the roadside as well as in gardens.

Most weeds, however, are native plants which prefer our well-dug and manured gardens to their natural homes on sand dunes, cliffs, and other steep rocks where fresh ground is always being exposed by land-slips. Many of the weeds are short-lived annuals which spring up from seed as soon as we dig our gardens. They scatter huge numbers of seeds and so there are always some ready to spring up. There are also some long-lived perennial weeds, such as the dock and the dandelion. The stinging nettle is another familiar perennial weed. Look at its stems and leaves under a hand lens to see the hairs that inject you with poison when you touch it.

Some common weeds are illustrated opposite. How many can you find in your garden? Explore your neighbourhood to see where they could have come from. If you live in a town, make a survey of a stretch of pavement or an old wall: look for weeds that have taken a foothold in cracks and crevices.

Plant Life on Walls

Explore old walls to find lichens – hardy little plants that often form circular patches on bricks and stones. Some are brightly coloured and people once collected them to make dyes for cloth. The lichens in the picture are map lichens, so called because their black-edged colonies often link up and then look like countries on a map. They occur in several different colours. Although lichens can grow in extremely cold and extremely hot and dry places, they cannot stand air pollution.

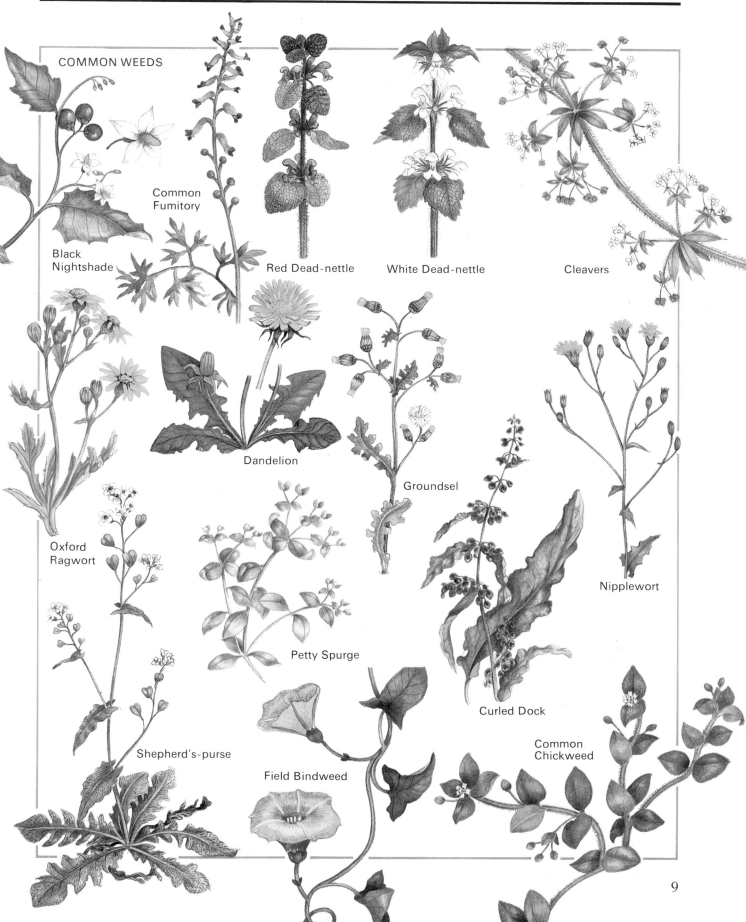

COMMON WEEDS

Black Nightshade

Common Fumitory

Red Dead-nettle

White Dead-nettle

Cleavers

Dandelion

Groundsel

Oxford Ragwort

Nipplewort

Petty Spurge

Curled Dock

Shepherd's-purse

Field Bindweed

Common Chickweed

Attracting Butterflies

A Butterfly Garden

No garden should be without the ice-plant, one of the best plants for attracting butterflies. Its domes of nectar-filled pink flowers open towards the end of summer and attract scores of butterflies, like the small tortoiseshells seen here with a red admiral. The small tortoiseshell sleeps through the winter and the ice-plant provides it with much of the food it needs to see it through this long sleep. A good butterfly garden will contain flowers from early spring until the last days of autumn, providing food for a wide range of butterflies.

Bring in the Butterflies

You can watch butterflies feeding at the flowers in the parks and gardens from early in the spring until well into the autumn. With the exception of the large and small whites, commonly known as cabbage whites, they are all welcome in the garden. As well as being beautiful to watch as they dance around the flowers, they help to pollinate the flowers, so that they produce seeds for the next year. Get as close as you can to some feeding butterflies and watch how they plunge their hair-like tongues into the flowers. The tongues are hollow and are used like drinking straws to suck up the sugary nectar. At the same time, pollen sticks on to the butterflies' legs and bodies and is carried from flower to flower. Watch how the butterfly coils its tongue up under its head when it has finished drinking.

A garden can be made especially attractive to butterflies by planting certain kinds of nectar-rich flowers. Aubretia is a good one for spring. Many people like to grow it on walls and in rock gardens. It is ideal for those butterflies that sleep through the winter and need food as soon as they wake up in the spring. Look out for small tortoiseshells, peacocks and brimstones on its flowers. Notice the very dark undersides of the tortoiseshells and peacocks. This helps to camouflage the insects during their winter sleep in hollow trees or in our sheds and attics. The brimstone prefers to sleep in a clump of ivy or a holly bush: see how its underside is green and leaf-like for good protection.

Good butterfly plants for later in the year include red valerian, lavender and the ice-plant pictured above. And don't forget the buddleia. This is often known as the butterfly bush, for its graceful purple flower spikes are thick with butterflies in the summer. Watch the butterflies closely to see what other kinds of flowers they like. They avoid the really big flowers because they can't reach the nectar. Notice how some species are happy to feed in large groups, while others prefer to be alone and tend to chase newcomers away.

You might like to try offering artificial foods to your garden butterflies. Put a solution of sugar and water in a bottle of the kind used for providing drinking water for pet mice (get this from your pet shop) and fix the bottle amongst the flowers. You may find butterflies feeding from it by day and moths by night.

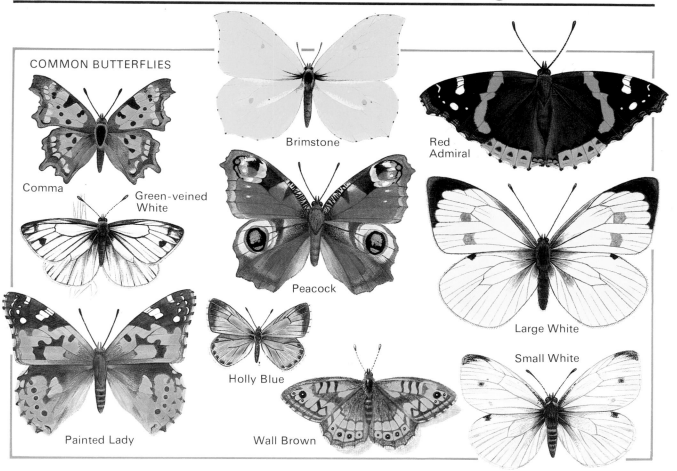

COMMON BUTTERFLIES

Comma

Brimstone

Red Admiral

Green-veined White

Peacock

Large White

Painted Lady

Holly Blue

Wall Brown

Small White

Some familiar garden butterflies are illustrated above. How many can you find in your garden or in your local park? Look at the comma's wings: they appear to have been torn, but the ragged appearance is quite natural. The underside is dark brown and the butterfly looks just like a dead leaf when it sleeps away the winter in the hedgerow. The green-veined white gets its name from the dark green lines on the underside. It is often blamed for destroying cabbages, but this is the work of its two cousins, the cabbage whites. The caterpillar of the green-veined white prefers to eat charlock, garlic mustard and other wild plants.

The Cabbage Whites

The large white butterfly looks very pretty as it sips nectar from the flowers, but its caterpillars destroy huge numbers of cabbages and related plants. Look for the clusters of yellow, skittle-shaped eggs under the leaves in August. The wise gardener will squash these eggs, but as a naturalist you might like to keep a batch to see what happens. The eggs hatch after a few days and the caterpillars start to feed. Give them fresh cabbage leaves every day and see how quickly they grow. Their strong smell and foul taste make them unacceptable to birds. After changing their skins several times they are ready to turn into pupae or chrysalises. They need upright surfaces for this and often choose fence posts or shed walls. Look for the speckled pupae in these places in the autumn. New butterflies emerge from them in the spring, but only a few ever get to this stage: most of the caterpillars are killed by parasitic insects which feed inside them. You will often find shrivelled caterpillars surrounded by the little yellow cocoons of these useful parasites.

The small white butterfly has a similar life history, but its caterpillars are green instead of black and yellow. They live singly while large white caterpillars spend their early life in dense colonies.

Bees and Wasps

The Buzzing of the Bees

As soon as the flowers open in spring they are visited by large furry bumble bees. These are queens that have just woken from their winter sleep. There are several different kinds: look for the different colour patterns. A few weeks later, when they have built up their strength on nectar, you will see them buzzing to and fro along the hedge bottoms in search of nesting sites on or under the ground. After a few weeks you will see some much smaller bees. These are the queens' first offspring, but they will not get any bigger. They are worker bees and they spend most of their time collecting pollen and nectar to feed bumble bee grubs back at the nest. Watch how they comb pollen from the body and pack it into the pollen baskets on the back legs: the baskets often bulge so much that the bees can hardly get airborne again. Don't be frightened to look closely: the bees won't hurt you.

The bumble bee is a social insect and several hundred adults may live in one nest.

Many other kinds of bees visit park and garden flowers and weeds, especially in spring. They are very important for pollinating the fruit trees. Most of them are solitary species, not living in large nests or colonies. Like the mason and digger wasps below, each female digs her own nest and provides food for her own young. There are no workers to look after the grubs as there are among the bumble bees and honey bees.

Watch the Wasps

Wasps also include both social and solitary species. The latter include many mason and digger wasps, but it is the social wasps that most of us notice in the garden, especially in late summer. Queen wasps appear a little later than bumble bee queens and they build their nests with paper which they make themselves

Bee and Wasp Nests

Mason Wasp

Digger Wasp

Small holes in brickwork are often the work of mason wasps, while digger wasps prefer to tunnel in the soil or in dead wood. The females of these insects work alone to dig out burrows for their young. Watch the entrance holes to see the insects bringing in small flies and other prey to stock their nests. Their grubs will eat this food later. Most of them take about a year to grow up and turn into new adults. The adults fly mainly in spring and summer.

Making a Bumble Bee Nest

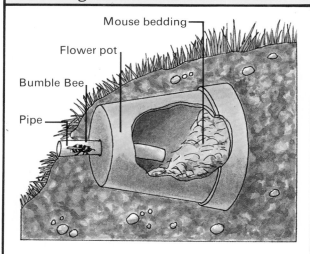

Mouse bedding

Flower pot

Bumble Bee

Pipe

Bumble bees often nest in old mouse holes. Encourage them to nest in your garden by providing an artificial home. All you need is a flower pot about 15 centimetres across, some old bedding from a pet mouse (or from a pet shop) and a piece of old pipe that fits the hole in the base of the pot. Bury the pot and bedding and poke through the pipe as shown above. With luck, a queen bee might find it a suitable place to build a nest.

by chewing wood into pulp. Their jaws scrape the wood from fence posts and many other objects, including dead hogweed stems, and it is quite a noisy business. You can hear it from several metres away on a still day.

The life history of the wasp colony is very much like that of the bumble bee colony, but the wasps feed their young on chewed-up insects instead of nectar and pollen. The wasps destroy lots of harmful insects during the summer, but they can become a nuisance themselves when their colonies break up in

Above: Hover-flies are often mistaken for wasps because of their black and yellow coats. Even birds make this mistake and leave the hover-flies alone, although the flies are actually harmless. If you look closely you will see that the hover-fly has only two wings. Wasps have four.

Below: The Colorado beetle is a very serious pest of potato crops on the continent. It came originally from North America.

The Garden Greenfly

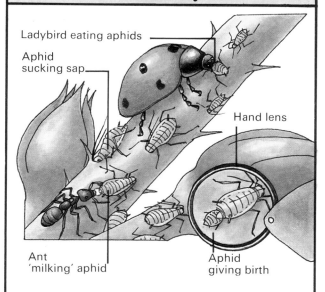

Ladybird eating aphids

Aphid sucking sap

Hand lens

Ant 'milking' aphid

Aphid giving birth

Examine the garden roses for greenfly in the spring. You are most likely to find these little insects, also known as aphids, clustering around the buds and young shoots. They dig their needle-like beaks into the plant and take out lots of sap for food. Most of the aphids are wingless in the spring, but you will find a few winged ones ready to fly to other plants. All are females at this time of the year and the adults can give birth to several babies every day. The young grow rapidly and soon have their own babies. In this way the aphid colony grows very quickly. Use your hand lens to look at the aphids and you might see one being born.

Several other insects live among the aphids. Ladybirds and their bluish grey grubs eat lots of them, but the aphids have their protectors as well. Look for ants roaming through the colony and stroking the aphids with their feelers. The ants are after honeydew, the sugary fluid which the aphids produce and which makes the plants sticky in the summer. The ants are so keen on the sweet honeydew that they guard the aphids and chase off intruders. Some ants even keep aphids like we keep cows. They take them into their nests and install them in special chambers with roots running through them. The aphids feed quite happily on the roots and when an ant wants a drink it merely goes up to an aphid and 'milks' it by stroking it gently.

Other Insects

the autumn. They spend their last few weeks feasting on ripe fruit and other sweet food. Notice how they fold their wings lengthwise, an easy way to distinguish the social wasps from the digger wasps. They may annoy you at the tea table, but they won't hurt you if you ignore them. Don't wave your arms around, for this will certainly make the wasps angry: and then they might sting. Like the queen bumble bee, the queen wasp sleeps through the winter and she wakes in the spring to form another colony.

Other Insects

Many people dislike earwigs, but these fierce-looking insects are quite harmless. They might nip with their pincers if you pick them up, but not hard enough to hurt you. They use the pincers to fight among themselves and also for defence against shrews and other animals that might try to eat them. The females have straighter and more slender pincers than the males. Earwigs are scavenging insects, eating almost anything when they come out at night. A good way to find them is to wrap an old cloth round the base of a tree trunk. The insects will congregate there and you can look at them in the morning.

Look out for the crane-flies or daddy-long-legs that are common in parks and gardens in late summer. They often buzz noisily around the house at night – try to catch one and examine it. Unlike most other insects, flies have only one pair of wings: the hind wings have been reduced to minute pin-like structures called balancers. They help the flies to fly straight. Notice that the male crane-fly has a swollen abdomen, while the female's is pointed at the tip. The females drive their abdomens into the ground to lay their eggs. Their grubs, known as leatherjackets, feed on the roots of grasses and other plants.

The Earthworm – a Valuable Friend

The famous naturalist Charles Darwin considered the earthworm to be one of the most important of all animals. It certainly plays a vital part in keeping the soil in good condition, and plants would not grow very well without it. There are thousands of worms in a hectare of soil, and they are especially common under grassland. Their tunnels help to drain the soil and provide air for plant roots. The animals also drag lots of dead leaves into the soil. Some of these are eaten but many are left to rot and enrich the

Life in a Forkful of Soil

Dig up a forkful of moist garden soil and examine it carefully on a board or a sheet of polythene. Some of the many kinds of animals that you might find in the soil are shown on the right. Wireworms are the grubs of slender beetles called click beetles. They eat plant roots and often tunnel into potatoes. Try spotting the difference between the carnivorous centipede and the vegetarian millipede by looking at the legs. Use a hand lens or magnifying glass to look for mites and other minute animals.

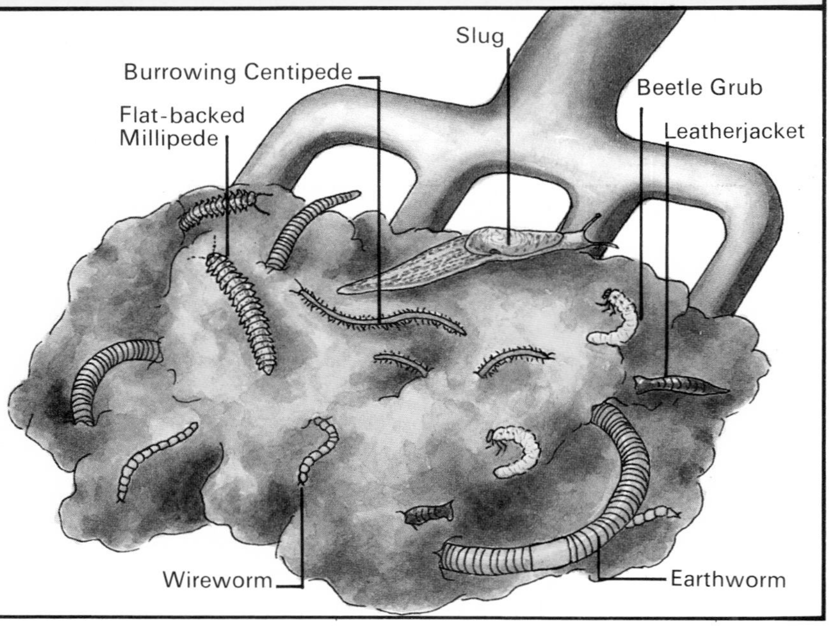

Slug
Burrowing Centipede
Flat-backed Millipede
Beetle Grub
Leatherjacket
Wireworm
Earthworm

soil. The worms also continuously mix the soil layers. They tunnel partly by swallowing the soil as they go and, after digesting any food material in it, they pass the soil out again as worm casts on or near the surface. In this way soil which has been swallowed in the deeper layers is regularly brought close to the surface. You can watch this ploughing action in a wormery like the one below. Only fine soil can be swallowed by the worms, and so in undisturbed places stones gradually sink as the worms take in soil from under them and deposit it on top.

Pick up a worm and try to work out which is its front end. Living in the soil, the animal has

Observing Snails

Trail can be made more visible by dusting with talcum powder

Snail rasping flesh from banana skin

Look for snails hiding in corners by day and mark their shells with blobs of paint. Search for them in the garden at night. How far have they travelled from home?

no need of eyes. It doesn't even have a real head, but the front end is more pointed than the rear and the worm will usually try to move towards the front. Run your fingers along the underside of the worm – the paler surface – and feel the tiny bristles which give it a grip as it moves through its tunnels. The same bristles also anchor it firmly if you try to pull a worm from its tunnel. Put the worm on a piece of paper and you will hear the bristles scraping. Try putting it on a piece of glass. It won't be able to move because it cannot dig in its bristles.

Look for worms on the ground on humid nights in the summer. You might see them dragging leaves into their burrows. If you disturb them they will shoot rapidly backwards and disappear, for they always keep the rear end firmly anchored in the burrow.

Ants Everywhere

Most parks and gardens contain ants. You might see their nests when digging in the garden or moving stones, but these little insects are not usually very conspicuous. On one day of the year, however, the nests 'explode' as thousands of flying ants swarm out and take to the air. This is the ants' marriage flight and all the nests in a given area usually erupt at the same time. After mating, the males die. Most of the females also perish – many are eaten by birds and other predators – but some females survive and either go back

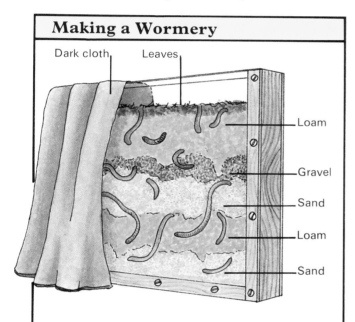

Making a Wormery

Dark cloth   Leaves

Loam
Gravel
Sand
Loam
Sand

This simple cage, consisting of two sheets of plastic about three centimetres apart in a wooden frame, will enable you to watch earthworms at work. Fill it with layers of different kinds of soil and add about six large worms. Drop some dead leaves or grass cuttings over the top as food for the worms and water well. Cover the wormery and examine it each day to see how the worms are getting on with their ploughing. Notice that the gravel layer gradually sinks as the worms remove the soil from beneath it. Look for worm casts on or near the surface of the soil.

Ants and Spiders

Keeping Ants

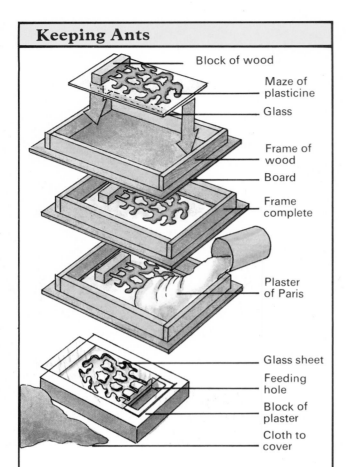

Block of wood

Maze of plasticine

Glass

Frame of wood

Board

Frame complete

Plaster of Paris

Glass sheet

Feeding hole

Block of plaster

Cloth to cover

Ants are easy to look after if you can make an escape-proof cage (formicarium) as shown above. Make sure the glass is about two centimetres smaller all round than the wooden frame: it should touch the frame only at the end opposite the wooden block. When the plaster has set, turn it upside-down and remove the wood and modelling wax. The plaster block now has a network of tunnels and a large hollow for a feeding area. Now go in search of ants. Wear gloves if you are after the red garden ants because these can sting. For a permanent colony you need the queen, who can be picked out by her much larger size. Put the ants in the formicarium and cover the tunnel area with a dark cloth. Slide the glass back a little to put fruit, honey and scraps of meat in the feeding area. Watch the ants come out to feed. Try giving them a stem thickly covered with aphids. Keep the tunnel area dark but examine it from time to time. Where does the queen take up residence to lay her eggs?

to their old nests to start laying eggs or they begin new colonies. Most of the ants in a colony are wingless workers. They are all daughters of the queen or queens and they do all the chores.

Our garden ants are omnivorous, eating lots of seeds and other plant matter as well as many other insects and other dead animals. But they are especially fond of sweet things and you will often see them collecting honeydew from aphids (see page 13). Put out some honey or a slice of orange in an area where you know there are ants. The workers will soon find it and you will see streams of them moving to and fro as they take the food back to the nest. Use a hand lens to watch the insects' jaws at work. There are two common garden species: the black ant, which even nests under town pavements, and the red ant. The black ant has no sting but the red ant, actually reddish-brown in colour, can give a painful sting.

Spiders in the Garden

Explore sunny flower beds and rockeries in spring and early summer and you may find small dark spiders sunbathing on the stones. These are wolf spiders. Instead of making webs, they chase after their insect prey. Try to catch one of the spiders in a glass tube. Look at it with your lens to see the large eyes — very necessary for a spider which relies on spotting prey from a distance and then running after it. You will sometimes see the females carrying their silken egg sacs at the rear end. When the eggs hatch the babies climb on to the mother's back and ride there for a few days, gradually falling off and becoming indepedent.

Many web-spinning spiders live in the garden. The garden spider, also known as the cross spider because of the markings on its back, is very common on bushes and fences. The webs that appear overnight on door and window frames usually belong to a greyish spider called *Zygiella x-notata*. Look closely at these webs and you will see that each has a triangular gap near the top. The spider hides in a nearby crevice and scampers down to the web when prey arrives. Try tickling the web with a piece of grass: you can sometimes fool the spider into thinking that its dinner has arrived – but not very often!

Life on a Wall

Brick and stone walls are readily colonized by animal life which takes to them just like natural rocks and cliffs. Old walls with soft and crumbling mortar are especially rich in wildlife because lots of plants can get a

Above: This Moorish gecko is a nocturnal lizard which hunts for insects on the walls in southern Europe. It often enters houses to hunt and can actually run across the ceiling. Notice its broad toes.

foothold here as well. Night is the best time for looking for animals on the wall, but keep your eyes open for the fascinating zebra spider in the sunshine. Its black and white pattern makes it hard to spot on lichen-covered walls. It is one of the jumping spiders, creeping slowly towards basking flies and then leaping on to them like a cat. Enormous eyes help it to judge distance very accurately. Search for the web of the spider *Segestria senoculata*: look carefully, for there is not much to see. The spider hides in a crevice and surrounds its lair with a number of trip-threads spreading out like the spokes of a wheel. When an insect stumbles over one of the threads the spider rushes out to catch it.

For night observations equip yourself with a strong torch. Woodlice are often very common on walls at night. Their skins are not waterproof and, like many other small animals, they come out at night because the air is moister then and there is less risk of drying up. In dry weather they keep nearer to the ground. Try to discover whether moonlight has any effect on them: do they stay lower down on moonlit nights? The woodlice feed on algae, pollen grains and other vegetable debris.

Life on a Wall

Old walls are very good places for finding small animals, especially if you look for them with a torch at night. Snails and woodlice browse on the algae and mosses, together with a host of very tiny insects. Numerous spiders make their homes in the crevices and either snare insects with webs or rush out to grab them. The long-legged house centipede also feeds on small insects. It lives mainly in the warmer parts of Europe but sometimes occurs in houses further north.

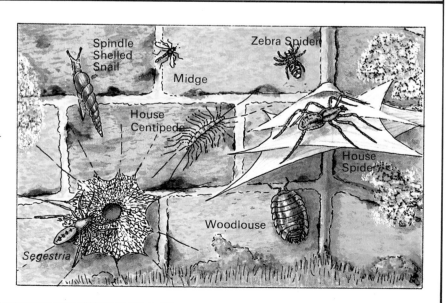

The Garden at Night

Centipedes hunt on the walls at night, catching flies and other insects that take a rest there. In southern Europe keep an eye open for the long-legged, speedy house centipede. It often comes indoors. You might even find scorpions hiding in crevices with their claws poking out to sieze passing prey.

Harvestmen are very common in the autumn, striding over the walls on their long legs and pouncing on a variety of small animals. They look rather like spiders, but if you study them carefully you will see that their bodies are not divided into two sections like the spiders. Harvestmen make no webs and have no poisonous fangs.

Observing at Night

As the sun sets in the evening, the butterflies seek shelter and the moths start to wake up. By dusk in the summer there are hundreds of moths floating and skimming through the garden. Take a torch and watch them feeding at the flowers. Some settle to take the nectar, while others may hover and feed with the aid of very long tongues. Some moths do not feed at all as adults, putting all their efforts into finding mates. Some familiar moths of parks and gardens are pictured below. The silver-Y flies in the daytime as well as by night. The eyed hawkmoth is well camouflaged when at rest on tree trunks by day, but if you disturb it it flashes the eye-like patterns on its hind wings. This frightens small birds, which think that the 'eyes' belong to a cat or an owl. You can find moths at all times of the year, but only a few are about in the winter.

Most moths are attracted to bright lights such as street lamps. Look at the lamps in your street on summer and autumn evenings and watch the moths crash to the ground or settle on nearby walls. Quite a number will come to your window if you leave the light on and the curtains undrawn. People who study moths make use of this attraction by putting out light-traps. These usually contain mercury-vapour lamps which give out lots of ultra-violet light. We can't see the ultra-violet, but moths certainly can. They spiral in to the lamp and fall through a funnel into the trap below. They can't escape and the entomologist – insect expert – can examine them and release them in the morning. You can buy a trap like this or make one: fix a strong light to a thin piece of wood and place this across a funnel poked into a cardboard box. If you can't make or buy a trap, try hanging a bright lamp over a white sheet. A camping light is ideal for this, but the beauty of a trap is that you can find out what moths visit your garden without staying up all night.

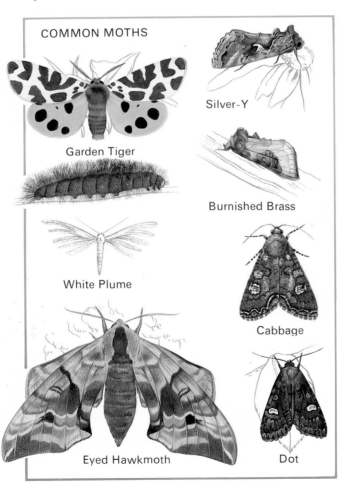

COMMON MOTHS

Garden Tiger

White Plume

Eyed Hawkmoth

Silver-Y

Burnished Brass

Cabbage

Dot

Acrobatic Bats

Bats start to fly at sunset and they catch huge numbers of moths and beetles during the night. Watch their amazingly agile flight as they twist and turn after insects against the darkening sky. They are the only mammals that can really fly. Their wings consist of flaps of skin running along the sides of the body and stretched across the incredibly long fingers. The bats are not blind, but their eyesight is poor and they rely on their powerful hearing to find their way and to catch food. As they plunge through the air they send out high-pitched sounds and listen for the echoes bouncing back from nearby objects. They know when the echoes are coming back from an insect and they change course to catch it. The insect is sometimes caught in the bat's mouth, but moths are more often scooped up in the wings.

Bats spend the daytime asleep, hanging upside-down in hollow trees, old buildings, roof spaces and similar places. Some even sleep amongst thick ivy. Our European bats, of which there are about 30 species, all go into hibernation through the winter months when there are simply not enough moths and other insects on the wing for them to eat.

The Hedgehog

The hedgehog is essentially a mammal of the hedgerow and the woodland edge but it finds our parks and gardens very much to its liking. It is a very common animal in many suburban areas. It spends the daytime asleep in rubbish heaps or in a leafy bed at the bottom of a hedge and comes out to feed at night. Together with the mole and the shrew, it belongs to a group known as the insectivores or insect-eaters, but it actually eats almost anything. It is very fond of earthworms and of the slugs and beetles that roam our gardens at night. Hedgehog droppings – often the first clue to the animals presence – are long and black and often full of beetle legs and wing-cases. There may also be pieces of centipede and earwig skeletons. Fruit is another important part of the hedgehog's diet, especially in the autumn when ripe fruit falls to the ground.

Above: A bat in flight. Notice the very long fingers supporting the wings. Notice also the large ears used for picking up the echoes, and the sharp insect-crushing teeth.

Right: Hedgehogs are good climbers. This one, showing its remarkably pig-like snout, has climbed a garden wall. To come down again it will just roll into a ball and drop to the ground. Notice there are no prickles underneath.

Garden Animals

Our lawns make fine courting grounds for the hedgehog. You might well have been woken up by the noisy performance in spring and summer as the male stomps round and round the female with much loud snorting and squealing. If you suspect that you have hedgehogs in or around your garden, try putting out some food for them. A bowl of cereal with some milk and dried fruit is ideal. The animals also like cat food. They are easy to watch and will come back night after night for food. Don't be tempted to take them indoors because they are loaded with fleas: the spines prevent them from grooming themselves like other animals.

Rats and Mice

The rats and mice belong to the large group of animals called rodents. They have chisel-like front teeth with which they can gnaw through all sorts of materials. The common or brown rat and the house mouse both came from Asia originally but are now found nearly all over the world. Both are very common in urban areas, indoors as well as out, and they do a lot of damage to food and other stores. In country areas these pests are found mainly around farms and rubbish dumps, although

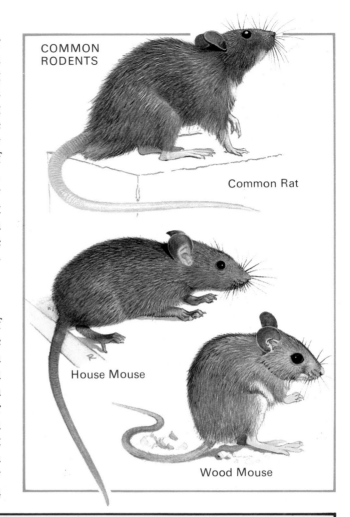

COMMON RODENTS

Common Rat

House Mouse

Wood Mouse

The Longworth Trap

The Longworth trap catches small mammals without hurting them. When the animals step on the trip-wire, the door drops down and imprisons them. Put some newspaper or other bedding in the trap to keep the animals warm at night. Bait is not necessary, but you can add some bread or grain and shrews will appreciate a lump of meaty cat food. Remember to check the trap regularly so that the animals do not go hungry. Release them after examination if you have nowhere to keep or feed them (see page 30).

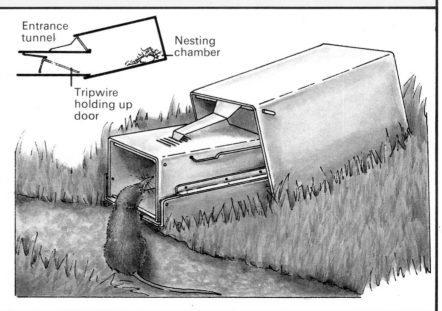

Entrance tunnel

Nesting chamber

Tripwire holding up door

Above: Foxes commonly come into gardens to look for food, even in the middle of towns. They often raid dustbins and this one has leapt on to a bird table in search of its supper.

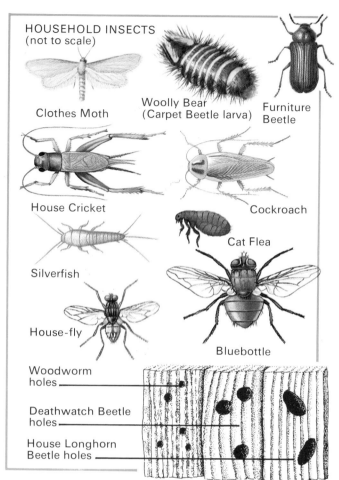

HOUSEHOLD INSECTS (not to scale)

Clothes Moth

Woolly Bear (Carpet Beetle larva)

Furniture Beetle

House Cricket

Cockroach

Cat Flea

Silverfish

House-fly

Bluebottle

Woodworm holes

Deathwatch Beetle holes

House Longhorn Beetle holes

the rat can travel many miles through open country, especially along river banks.

The wood mouse often lives in gardens, in towns as well as in country areas, and often comes into houses where there are no house mice to compete with it. It has larger eyes and ears and much larger feet than the house mouse. Woodmice generally nest just under the ground and make runways all over their territories. Look for their food stores in and under sheds and in log piles. The stores contain various nuts, cherry pips, dried hawthorn fruits and assorted seeds. By the end of winter most of these stores have been used up and only empty shells remain.

Insects in the House

The illustrations above right show a few of the many insects that can be found in houses and other buildings. You will find many more if you search cupboards and neglected corners. Some, like the small flies that swarm over the window panes, are accidental prisoners, but many others take up permanent residence in our buildings and do a great deal of harm. The grubs of clothes moths and carpet beetles chew through woollen clothes and carpets. Cockroaches and crickets eat all kinds of foods. The cat flea sucks blood from our household pets and often has a go at us as well. Bluebottles and houseflies both carry disease germs to food. Bluebottles also lay their eggs on meat and fish and their grubs quickly eat through the food. Silverfish are primitive wingless insects covered with minute silvery scales. Try picking one up – if you can catch it – and you will find the scales all over your fingers. These insects feed on spilt flour and other scraps and don't do much harm, although they sometimes damage books and wallpaper.

Even rafters, floor boards and wooden furniture are not safe from insect attack. The grubs of the furniture beetle or woodworm chew through all kinds of wood and the adult beetles leave the familiar tell-tale holes as they leave. By then the damage has been done.

Garden Ponds

Making a Garden Pond

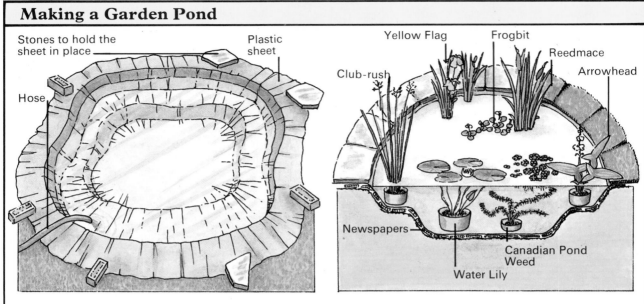

Stones to hold the sheet in place — Plastic sheet

Hose

Yellow Flag — Frogbit

Club-rush — Reedmace — Arrowhead

Newspapers — Canadian Pond Weed — Water Lily

Use black polythene or a special pond liner to make a pond of any shape you like. Dig the hole to a depth of at least 60 centimetres in the centre and leave a shallow ledge around the edge. Put a layer of newspaper or soft sand in the bottom to protect the liner from any sharp stones and then stretch the liner across the hole. Hold the edges down with a few large stones and then start to fill your pond. Watch the liner gradually stretch and mould itself to the shape of the hole. The plants are best kept in pots. Put the ones that like shallow water on the ledges. Finish off the edge with stone or turf, making sure that you have an area of sloping bank where newts and other creatures can crawl out.

Deathwatch beetles don't normally invade ordinary houses. They like very old oak and are most often found in churches. In the wild these beetles all play a useful role in getting rid of dead trees

A Garden Pond

Garden ponds can be a lot of fun for the naturalist, and are very important for wildlife. As streams become polluted and many old farm and village ponds are filled in, garden ponds are taking over as major homes for frogs and toads and many other water-loving animals. Try to get a pond installed in your garden. It is not a difficult job. You can buy ready-shaped glass fibre ponds which are merely dropped into holes dug to the same shape. Alternatively, you can use a flexible liner as shown above. The pond need not be very large, but try to make it at least a metre across. Planted with a variety of native water plants, it will soon look quite natural. Buy your plants from a garden centre or get them from pond-owning friends: never dig them up from the wild.

Frogs, toads and newts will all find your pond and may well breed there. Many water-loving insects will also set up home in the pond. Look for water beetles scurrying amongst the submerged plants and coming up for air every now and then. Pond skaters may skim about on the surface, darting about after small flies that fall into the water. Watch the water snails gliding over the plants. They help to keep down the fluffy green algae that build up around the sides of the pond, but too many snails will destroy the pond plants. Dragonflies may swoop to and fro over a fairly large pond, streaking after the small midges that congregate there. Swallows and martins may even come to gather mud for nest-building. You can add goldfish if you like, but they will eat many of the other animals. They may themselves be eaten by a visiting heron.

The Naturalist at Work

As soon as you start to explore the world outside you will meet hundreds of different kinds of plants and animals and you will want to know the names of some of them. The larger and more colourful things, including trees, mammals and birds, and most flowers and butterflies, can be identified quite easily with the help of good guide books.

But guide books can't tell you everything and the best way to get to know your local countryside and its wildlife is to join your local natural history society or naturalists' trust. These groups normally organize excursions, during which you can explore under the guidance of expert naturalists. You will be able to learn the names of the plants and animals around you, and also pick up lots of tips on how to identify things from brief glimpses or even just snatches of songs.

A Better View

You don't need a lot of equipment for exploring the countryside, but most naturalists find that they need binoculars sooner or later, especially if they are studying birds or mammals. There are many models on the market and it is important to choose a pair that suits your particular purpose. If you look at a pair of binoculars you will see two numbers marked on them: 8 x 30 is a typical example, indicating that the binoculars magnify things eight times and that the objective lenses – those furthest from your eyes – are 30 millimetres in diameter. The size of the objective lenses has nothing to do with the magnification of the binoculars, but it does control the amount of light passing through them. Small objectives allow less light through than large ones and binoculars of this type are therefore not very good in dim light. If you want to watch birds or mammals at dusk or at night you should choose a pair with large objectives.

Binocular magnifications generally range from about x 6 – the smallest to be of any real use – to about x 12. You might be tempted to go for the highest magnification, but this is a mistake unless you are interested only in seabirds or mountain animals, which are usually a long way away. Powerful binoculars cannot be focused on objects less than about

The Home Laboratory

You will undoubtedly collect all kinds of specimens while exploring the countryside – pressed flowers, bark rubbings, sea shells and many other oddments. You will also have various pieces of equipment, including your binoculars. It is a good idea to keep all these things together. Try to get a table or desk specially for this purpose – a sort of home laboratory where you can study your collections. A good light is necessary, especially if you are using a microscope. The same light can be used for warming a vivarium if you have one.

Binoculars and Microscopes

Choosing Binoculars

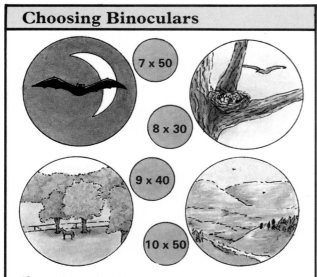

7 x 50

8 x 30

9 x 40

10 x 50

If you intend using binoculars mainly at night you should choose 7 x 50 or 8 x 50, but for normal daytime use choose 8 x 30, 8 x 40 or 9 x 40. Powerful 10 x 50 binoculars are good for observing distant scenes. Clean the lenses when necessary with special tissues.

eight metres away, and so you might not be able to study the birds on your bird table. Until recently, powerful binoculars were also large and heavy and very tiring to carry around all day. Improvements in design have overcome this problem, but powerful light-weight binoculars are still rather expensive. The ordinary naturalist can manage perfectly well with less powerful equipment. Always choose the best you can afford within the size and magnification range that you need (see above), and make sure that you try the binoculars before buying them. Do they feel comfortable at your eyes? Are they too heavy to carry for long periods? Do they focus smoothly? Take them outside the shop and focus on buildings at different distances. Is everything sharp and clear?

A Closer Look

If you want to study the smaller plants and animals, or to make a detailed examination of flowers, you will certainly need some kind of magnifying glass. The most convenient kind for use in the countryside is a hand lens. You can buy these pocket lenses quite cheaply, with a choice of magnifications. For general use a x10 lens is the most suitable. Use it together with good guide books and it will help you to identify numerous insects, spiders, mosses and other small organisms. Tie your lens to a piece of string and keep it round your neck while you are out: it will be easy to get at and you won't leave it behind.

Below: Using a simple hand lens to study the structure of a clover flower-head. You will be surprised how much detail it reveals.

Choosing a Microscope

A microscope is not essential for the amateur naturalist, but it will enable you to identify many small creatures, especially those living in soil and leaf litter. Like the hand lens, it also opens up a world of beautiful and complex patterns and amazing detail. If you are lucky enough to have a microscope you will undoubtedly spend many hours gathering and gazing at insects and other small animals, shells, leaves and an assortment of sand grains and other materials.

Microscopes are of two main kinds: monocular microscopes, with a single eye-piece, and binocular microscopes with two eye-pieces. Monocular microscopes generally magnify things 100 times or more and are used mainly for examining minute pieces of animals or plants. A simple microscope of this kind costs only a few pounds and would make a nice birthday present. Binocular microscopes are more expensive but you can sometimes find second-hand ones. Low-power binocular microscopes, magnifying about 30 times, have the advantage of space between the body of the microscope and the object you are looking at. You can even examine live insects under it – something that you can't do with a monocular model unless the animals are extremely small.

Photographing Nature

Most naturalists like to take photographs of the various sorts of countryside and of the plants and animals that live there. It is the ideal way to build up a record of the changes occurring in a particular place from season to season and, if done carefully, it causes no harm to the plants and animals. The wildlife photographer normally chooses a single-lens reflex camera with a detachable lens. The reflex arrangement, consisting of a mirror and various prisms, allows you to see *exactly* what the camera lens is seeing, so that you can compose your picture properly without chopping off the top of a flower or the head of an animal. The detachable lens allows you to put extension tubes between it and the camera body for close-up pictures, and also allows you to use different lenses for different effects. A telephoto lens, for example, works like a telescope, enlarging part of the view so that objects come out larger in the final picture. A wide-angle lens works the other way: each object appears smaller in the final picture but, because the lens covers a wider field, you get much more of the landscape in your picture.

A complete outfit for wildlife photography is very expensive, but you don't have to buy everything at once. Decide on one of the well-known makes of 35 mm SLR cameras and then you can build up your outfit gradually, getting thoroughly familiar with each piece of equipment as you get it. If possible, choose a camera with a built-in exposure meter which

The Binocular Microscope

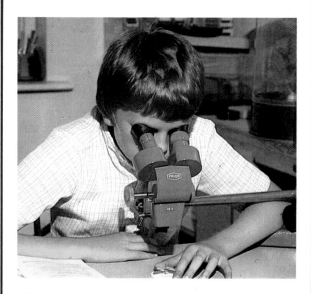

Binocular microscopes with a magnification of between 30 and 50 times are ideal for looking at and identifying small insects. The distance between the microscope and the object means you can use tweezers or a needle to move legs and wings or to turn the whole animal over. Always work in a good light when using a microscope.

Below: Binoculars are not just for looking at distant objects. Here they are being used to watch large spiders on the far side of a ditch.

measures the amount of light actually coming through the lens. The camera will then indicate the right exposure no matter what lens or other attachment you are using, but there is one important thing to remember if you are photographing scenes with lots of sky or snow in them. The exposure meter will be unduly affected by the bright areas and the landscape will come out too dark unless you adjust the camera setting.

To start with, all you need is the camera body equipped with a standard lens and a skylight filter. The filter is especially important in the mountains or by the sea, where there is lots of ultra-violet light. Without it, the ultra-violet gets through to the film and makes the pictures too blue. A standard lens is fine for general landscapes, trees, groups of flowers and large animals. A sturdy tripod

should be high on your list. It holds the camera steady and allows you to make long exposures without risk of camera-shake. This is especially useful in landscape photography, where the long exposure and small aperture give you sharpness throughout the picture.

The next most useful piece of equipment is a telephoto lens. Using the standard lens, a sparrow photographed from only three metres away would still fill only a very small part of your picture. A 200 mm telephoto lens is useful for photographing birds on a bird-table, but for birds in the wild you really need a lens of at least 400 mm focal length.

Taking Close-ups

If you want to photograph insects or take close-ups of flowers you will need some close-up accessories. Extension tubes, which fit between the lens and the camera body, are the most convenient. You will usually find that you need extra light for close-up photography, and this means attaching a small electronic flash. Many photographers prefer two flashes linked together so that they fire

Above left: Flowers, photographed with a large aperture to throw the surroundings out of focus.

Left: Wide-angle lenses are good for scenery as they take in a large area. The photograph, left, was taken with a 35 mm lens and includes the stream as well as the mountain. The picture above was taken from exactly the same spot, but with a 200 mm telephoto lens. This acts like a telescope, magnifying just a small part of the scene – in this case the heather in the centre.

Wildlife Photography

Right: The author at work on a close-up photograph of a flower using a simple flash-gun to provide extra light. Two or even three flash-guns are sometimes required for certain pictures. You might have to get into very awkward positions to take close-up pictures, but always take care not to damage surrounding vegetation.

Speeds and Stop Numbers

Cameras normally have two movable rings engraved with numbers. Together, they control the amount of light entering the camera. Too little or too much light falling on the film will spoil the picture. One ring controls the speed at which the shutter opens and closes, and in a typical camera it may range from half a second to 1/500th second. Don't use speeds slower (longer) than 1/60th second without a tripod or you may get blurred pictures through camera shake. The second ring controls the size of the aperture through which light gets into the camera. It is generally marked from about 2·8 to 16 or 22. The larger the number, the smaller the aperture. A small aperture gives a good depth of field, with everything nice and sharp from the foreground into the far distance. To make up for the small aperture, however, you must give a longer exposure so that the right amount of light reaches the film. A large aperture gives only a shallow depth of field: if the foreground is in focus the background will be blurred, and vice-versa. This is often useful if you want to make a bird or a flower stand out from the background. Large apertures go with short exposures, and the latter are also needed to 'freeze' moving subjects.

simultaneously. This reduces the shadows caused by a single flash. You can achieve a similar result with a sheet of white paper on one side to reflect the light into the shadow areas. Unless you have the very latest automatic equipment, you must experiment at first to find out just how far away the flash must be for the correct exposure. In all close-up photography you must work with small apertures to get enough depth of field.

Remember the Rules

Naturalists and photographers have devised a set of rules for wildlife photography. Designed to protect our wildlife, these rules can be summed up by stating that the welfare of the subject is more important than the photograph. Remember this when you are photographing plants and animals. Don't trample on other flowers to get a good picture of one specimen, and don't pull up plants that might be in your way – although you can certainly bend the stalks gently out of the way while taking your pictures: tent pegs are useful for holding grasses back in this way. Leave the place as you found it, and always ask permission if you want to photograph something on private land. Remember that it is against the law to disturb nesting birds.

Watching Birds and Mammals

A Hide for Watching Birds

Most wild birds are shy and timid and it is difficult to watch them properly without some kind of camouflage. If they can't see you they will act normally and may come quite close. It is sometimes sufficient to hide behind trees and bushes, but these are not always available. Bird photographers, who often have to sit for hours or even days to get their pictures, make artificial hides – sometimes very elaborate ones high in the trees.

Making a Hide

Green and brown cover

Stool

Viewing holes

Make a frame from eight strong canes or straight branches lashed together with string at the top. Cut an old sheet painted green and brown into two rectangles and sew them together into a large bag to fit neatly over the top and sides. Sew in a piece of plastic under the top to make it waterproof and make a flap in one side for an entrance. Cover the hide with a few leafy branches for extra camouflage and make peep-holes in one side at the right height for comfortable viewing. Make one for your camera if you want to take photographs. The hide shown here is cut away to show the interior with its folding stool. If watching a nest, make sure that you don't disturb the birds while setting up your hide.

For everyday bird-watching, you can make a simple hide with a couple of stout canes and an old sheet dyed or painted brown and green to match the surroundings. Fix the sheet to the canes and sit or stand behind it. This is a very practical hide if you want to watch birds in a particular spot – birds coming to and from a nest box, for example.

But if you want to watch birds all around you, a hide like the one on the left is necessary. Such a hide is ideal for regular bird-watching in a large garden or on other private land where it can be left in position so that the birds get used to it. Farmers and other land owners are usually quite happy for you to set up a hide on their land, but remember to ask their permission first. Unfortunately, you can't leave a hide safely in parks or on commons and other public spaces, and you can't rebuild it every time you want to use it because this would frighten the birds away. The answer here is to use a mobile hide, carried in front of you like a shield. A folding clothes airer with a camouflaged sheet draped over it works quite well, but you can make a lighter frame with a few strips of wood. The hide can be erected in an instant with no disturbance to the surroundings, and you can also creep forward with it.

Hides and Mammals

You can also use your hide to observe mammals, such as deer, although hides are not really necessary for mammal-watching. Mammals generally have poorer eyesight than birds and, as long as you keep still, they probably won't notice you. The advantage of a hide is that you can shuffle about behind it without disturbing the animals. The really important thing is to be downwind of the animals, so that the wind does not carry your scent or your sounds to them: most mammals rely on scents and sounds to warn them of danger. The mobile hide is obviously the one to use, because you can then adjust your position according to the wind direction. Get to know the habits of your local deer: they usually follow definite routes each day and have favourite resting places, and when you have discovered these you will be able to watch them much more easily. Look for their characteristic footprints, known as slots, to show you where the deer gather.

A Nest Box for your Garden

If you have enjoyed feeding the birds in your garden in the winter, encourage some of them to stay around for the spring and summer by putting up a few nest boxes. You can buy ready-made boxes from pet shops and garden centres, or you can make them yourself. Don't worry about a few gaps or rough edges. The gaps will actually aid ventilation.

The tit-box, with a small hole in the side or front, is the most popular kind of nest box. You can make one from a log or from a single plank of wood (see right). Such a box will attract blue tits, coal tits and great tits. Tree sparrows, nuthatches and tree creepers will also move into nest boxes of this kind, and if you make sure that the entrance hole is no more than 29 millimetres across you will keep out the house sparrow. The birds that use these boxes normally nest in holes in the tree trunks, and so you need not hide the nest box away in the branches. You can fix it to a tree trunk or a fence or a wall so that you can get a good view of the birds, but it must be out of the reach of cats and not in the full sun. The box need not be on a vertical surface, but if it does slope make sure that the entrance faces downwards so that the rain does not get in. Robins, spotted flycatchers and many other small birds prefer open-fronted boxes, sited in more protected places, such as walls or tree trunks covered with climbing plants.

If you have a suitable shed or fence you might be able to set up an observation nest box. This is made from a plank in the normal way, but the back is made from a sheet of clear glass or plastic and the box is then fitted against a hole in the shed or fence so that you can look through the back.

All nest boxes should be in position well before the nesting season so that the birds can explore them thoroughly and get used to them. Watch the birds choosing their homes and gathering nesting material for them.

Making a Nest Box

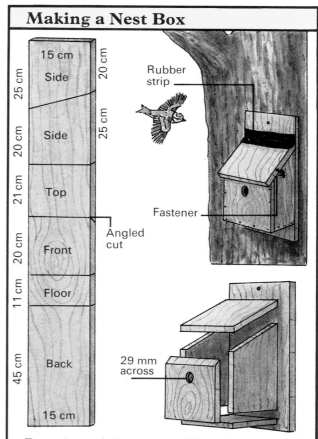

To make a tit-box, you will need a plank of wood, a strip of rubber inner tube, some nails or screws and a fastener. Cut the plank into two sections as shown in the diagram. Drill an entrance hole (29 mm in diameter) in the front section and a few small drainage holes in the floor section. Nail the strip of rubber to the lid and back to form the hinge and then nail or screw the sections together. Fit the catch to the side. An open-fronted nest box can be made in the same way but it needs only half of the front section and no hinged lid.

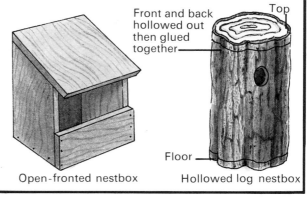

Open-fronted nestbox   Hollowed log nestbox

A simple Vivarium

Don't be tempted to open the boxes to see how the birds are getting on: the hinged lids are for cleaning out the boxes in the autumn.

Remember that most birds are strongly territorial in the breeding season, with each pair defending a particular area. A small garden is not likely to support more than one pair of each kind, so don't waste your money on lots of boxes: two tit-boxes and two open-fronted kinds are plenty for a small garden

A Simple Vivarium

A vivarium is merely an artificial home for land animals, just as an aquarium is a home for water-living creatures. You can use it for keeping lizards and snakes, frogs and toads, and small mammals, such as mice and voles.

Think carefully before deciding to set up a vivarium: can you provide enough of the correct food for your charges? This is especially important with the reptiles and amphibians, for these generally need live animals to eat. You will need lots of flies, slugs and worms to keep frogs and toads happy, although you might be able to tempt them with small pieces of meat dangled in front of them on pieces of cotton. Lizards also eat slugs and insects. The maggots or gentles sold for fishing bait are a good form of insect food. Feeding snakes is much more difficult:

Set up a Vivarium

Vivaria are often sold in pet shops, but these tend to be made of metal and they are not really suitable because it is not easy to see what is happening inside. An old fish tank makes a very good vivarium, and it doesn't matter if it leaks. Fit a cover of perforated zinc or fine wire mesh. Strong wooden boxes can be used if you turn them on their sides and put a glass or plastic window across the front. They also need ventilation panels made of perforated zinc. You can often find old cupboards in junk shops which may be right for conversion to vivaria. The best size is about 50 centimetres long, 30 centimetres wide and 50 centimetres high. This vivarium houses frogs and toads.

although they catch mice and frogs and other backboned animals in the wild, it is illegal to give them live prey of this kind in captivity. If they will not eat insects you must train them to eat freshly-killed food. Snake-keeping is really for the experts.

How you furnish your vivarium depends very much on what animals you are going to keep. Lizards need a layer of gravel on the bottom and a few logs or rocks on which to bask. A small dead branch will give them something else to scamper over, and the animals might like a small piece of turf to explore. You can put a fresh piece of turf in every week or two. Drinking water is important and can be provided in a small pond made from a shallow pie dish. A similar set-up will satisfy mice and voles, but arrange the rocks or logs to form a sleeping chamber. Give voles lots of turf to nibble and tunnel in.

Frogs and toads require moister conditions and you should cover the gravel with a layer of damp peat or moss. Give them a fair-sized pool to bathe in. If your vivarium is made from a fish tank and still holds water, you can put an inch or two in the bottom and then build up the rocks and branches, but this arrangement is less easy to clean out than one in which the 'pond' is in a separate dish. It is very important to keep the vivarium clean.

All the cold-blooded animals – the reptiles and the amphibians – appreciate some extra warmth and you can provide this by shining a reading lamp into the vivarium for a few hours each day. A 40-watt bulb is sufficient for the animals to 'sunbathe'.

Simple Sound Recording

If you have a small cassette tape recorder you can try making recordings of birds and other animals, including grasshoppers and crickets. A tape recorder with a manual recording level control will produce better results than one with an automatic control. The slender stick microphones that come with most cassette recorders are quite good, but you will get better results with a slightly more expensive microphone. Be sure to get a low impedance microphone, which will allow you to use a

Sound Recording

Before making a sound recording, identify the animal you are recording and look for the best possible position to record it from without disturbing it. Here a cricket in a tree is being recorded with a simple microphone tied to a stick. The microphone is shielded from wind noise by gauze wrapped around a wire frame. This creates a zone of still air around the microphone. Hides are useful for recording birds and other animals.

long lead and get the recorder well away from the microphone. Then you won't hear the hum of the motor. Try not to hold the microphone in your hand, for it will pick up the slightest movement of your fingers: it is a good idea to bind or clip the microphone to a long stick. Always use headphones to hear exactly what you are picking up.

When using a stick microphone you usually have to put it very close to the sound you are recording. Try attaching it to a bird table in the garden: with a long lead you can hide indoors and listen to what is happening. Or put your microphone in a flower bed to pick up the sounds of the visiting bees. Add a brief commentary after each item so that you will not forget what each recording is.

Index

Page numbers in *italics* refer to illustrations

Editor: Vanessa Clarke
Designer: Ben White
Illustrators: Wendy Brammall, Martin Camm, Jeane Colville, Alan Male, Bernard Robinson, Ann Winterbotham and David Wright.
Cover Design: Pinpoint Design Company
Picture Research: Jackie Cookson

Photographs: page 6 Heather Angel; 19 NHPA *centre*, Pat Morris *bottom right*; 21 NHPA; 30 Heather Angel; all other photographs: Michael Chinery.

First published in 1985 by Kingfisher Books Limited, Elsley Court, 20-22 Great Titchfield Street, London W1P 7AD
A Grisewood & Dempsey Company

Text Copyright © Michael Chinery 1985
Illustrations Copyright © Kingfisher Books Ltd 1985

BRITISH LIBRARY CATALOGUING IN PUBLICATION DATA
Chinery, Michael
    Parks and Gardens.–(Exploring the countryside)
    1. Natural history–Great Britain–Juvenile literature 2. Garden fauna–Great Britain–Juvenile literature 3. Parks–Great Britain–Juvenile literature
    I. Title   II. Series
    574.941   QH137

ISBN: 0 86272 150 4

Phototypeset by Southern Positives and Negatives (SPAN), Lingfield, Surrey
Printed in Italy by Vallardi Industrie Grafiche, Milan